How do I use this scheme?

Key Words with Peter and Jane has three
parallel series, each containing twelve books. All three
series are written using the same carefully controlled
vocabulary. Readers will get the most out of **Key Words** with
Peter and Jane when they follow the books in the pattern
1a, 1b, 1c; 2a, 2b, 2c and so on.

• Series a
gradually introduces and repeats new words.

• Series b
provides further practice of these same words, but
in a different context and with different illustrations.

• Series c
uses familiar words to teach **phonics** in a methodical way,
enabling children to read increasingly difficult words.
It also provides a link to writing.

LADYBIRD BOOKS

UK | USA | Canada | Ireland | Australia
India | New Zealand | South Africa

Ladybird Books is part of the Penguin Random House group of companies
whose addresses can be found at global.penguinrandomhouse.com.

www.penguin.co.uk   www.puffin.co.uk   www.ladybird.co.uk

First published 1964
This edition 2009, 2014, 2016
Copyright © Ladybird Books Ltd, 1964
001

A CIP catalogue record for this book is
available from the British Library

ISBN: 978-1-409-30143-1

Printed in China

Key Words

with Peter and Jane

1b

Look at this

written by W. Murray
illustrated by J.H. Wingfield

Jane and Peter

Jane   and   Peter

Peter and Jane.

I like Peter
and Jane.

I like

Jane likes Peter

and

Peter likes Jane

Peter and Jane like the dog.

I like the dog.

---

the   The   dog

Peter likes trees

and

Jane likes trees

---

trees

A shop.
I like shops.

A   a   shop   shops

Jane is in

a shop

and

Peter is in

a shop.

---

is in

Here is a ball
in a shop.
Jane likes
the ball.

Here   here   ball

Jane has
the dog
and
Jane has
the ball.

---

has

The dog has the ball.

The dog likes the ball.

Jane has

a shop.

Here is

Jane's shop.

The shop

has toys.

Jane's shop

is a

toy shop.

---

toy   toys

Here is
a toy dog
in Jane's shop

Here is

a tree

in Jane's shop

Peter is in
Jane's shop.
The dog is in
the shop.

Here is Peter

and

here is Jane.

Here is a tree.

Peter and Jane

like the tree.

The dog is here

Jane likes toys

and

Peter likes toys

The toy dog
is in the tree.
The ball
is in the tree.

The dog has a toy.
The dog likes toys.

I like
the tree.
I like toys.

Here is Peter's toy and here is Jane's toy.

Jane likes the toy and Peter likes the toy.

New words used in this book

Total number of new words: 16
Average repetition per word: 12